Brotherhood of Railroad Trainmen, Petitioner, v. Chicago, Milwaukee, St. Paul and Pacific Railroad Company, et al. U.S. Supreme Court Transcript of Record with Supporting Pleadings

DAVID LEO UELMEN, JAMES P REEDY, RALPH S SPRITZER

Brotherhood of Railroad Trainmen, Petitioner, v. Chicago, Milwaukee, St. Paul and Pacific Railroad Company, et al.

Petition / DAVID LEO UELMEN / 1967 / 620 / 389 U.S. 933 / 88 S.Ct. 298 / 19 L.Ed.2d 286 / 9-15-1967
Brotherhood of Railroad Trainmen, Petitioner, v. Chicago, Milwaukee, St. Paul and Pacific Railroad Company, et al.
Brief in Opposition (P) / JAMES P REEDY / 1967 / 620 / 389 U.S. 933 / 88 S.Ct. 298 / 19 L.Ed.2d 286 / 10-13-1967
Brotherhood of Railroad Trainmen, Petitioner, v. Chicago, Milwaukee, St. Paul and Pacific Railroad Company, et al.
Memorandum (P) / RALPH S SPRITZER / 1967 / 620 / 389 U.S. 933 / 88 S.Ct. 298 / 19 L.Ed.2d 286 / 10-18-1967

Brotherhood of Railroad Trainmen, Petitioner,
v. Chicago, Milwaukee, St. Paul and Pacific
Railroad Company, et al. U.S. Supreme Court
Transcript of Record with Supporting Pleadings

Table of Contents

Office-Supreme Court, U.S.
FILED

SEP 1 5 1967

JOHN F. DAVIS, CLERK

IN THE

Supreme Court of the United States

OCTOBER TERM, 1967

No. 620

388

BROTHERHOOD OF RAILROAD TRAINMEN, *Petitioner,*

v.

CHICAGO, MILWAUKEE, ST. PAUL AND PACIFIC RAILROAD COMPANY, ET AL., *Respondents.*

PETITION FOR A WRIT OF CERTIORARI TO THE UNITED STATES COURT OF APPEALS FOR THE DISTRICT OF COLUMBIA CIRCUIT

GOLDBERG, PREVIANT & UELMEN
   511 Warner Theatre Building
   Milwaukee, Wisconsin 53203

DAVID LEO UELMEN

SCHOENE and KRAMER
   1625 K Street, N.W.
   Washington, D. C. 20006

MILTON KRAMER

Attorneys for Petitioner

September, 1967

PRESS OF BYRON S. ADAMS PRINTING, INC., WASHINGTON, D. C.

INDEX

CITATIONS

IN THE

Supreme Court of the United States

OCTOBER TERM, 1967

———

No.

———

BROTHERHOOD OF RAILROAD TRAINMEN, *Petitioner,*

v.

CHICAGO, MILWAUKEE, ST. PAUL AND PACIFIC RAILROAD
COMPANY, ET AL., *Respondents.*

———

PETITION FOR A WRIT OF CERTIORARI TO THE UNITED STATES COURT OF APPEALS FOR THE DISTRICT OF COLUMBIA CIRCUIT

———

The Brotherhood of Railroad Trainmen prays that a writ of certiorari issue to review the judgment of the United States Court of Appeals for the District of Columbia Circuit entered in this case on July 27, 1967.

OPINIONS BELOW

The opinion of the District Court (J.A. 38-39)[1] has not been reported officially or unofficially and is appended hereto as Appendix A. The opinion of the Court of Appeals (Appendix B) has not yet been officially reported. It is unofficially reported at 65 LRRM 2965.

JURISDICTION

The judgment of the Court of Appeals was dated and entered on July 27, 1967, and is appended hereto as Appendix C. The jurisdiction of this Court is invoked under 28 U.S.C. Section 1254(1).

QUESTIONS PRESENTED

1. Whether that part of the railroad "work rules" arbitration, ordered by Congress in Public Law 88-108, which was delegated by the arbitration board [No. 282] established by Congress in that Act to special boards of adjustment, was required to be conducted by such special boards in accordance with the procedures and within the procedural restrictions prescribed by Congress for the conduct of the arbitration, i.e., whether such special boards of adjustment were required to conduct the arbitration delegated to them in accordance with the procedures of Sections 7 and 8 of the Railway Labor Act to the extent Board 282 was required to do so.

---

[1] "J.A." refers to the printed joint appendix filed in the Court of Appeals. "R" refers to the transcript of evidentiary proceedings in four volumes, filed in the Court of Appeals, which was not printed in the joint appendix. "Pltf. Ex." refers to exhibits which were filed in the Court of Appeals in the form of an exhibit book, and not printed in the joint appendix. The transcript and exhibit book, although not printed, were made a part of the joint appendix.

2. Whether the judgment in *Brotherhood of Locomotive Firemen and Enginemen* v. *Chicago, Burlington & Quincy R. Co.*, 225 F. Supp. 11 (D.D.C. 1964), *aff'd* 331 F. 2d 1020 (D.C. Cir. 1964), *cert. denied*, 337 U.S. 918 (1964), prior to the establishment of any such special boards of adjustment or the commencement of any of their proceedings, and prior to any issue having arisen concerning what procedural requirements are applicable to such special boards, is *res judicata* of Question No. 1.

3. Whether Board 282, consistent with P.L. 88-108, may interpret its award to permit the special boards of adjustment it created: (1) to deny the request of one party that a complete record, including a transcript, of the proceedings be maintained; (2) to enter an award without making any findings setting forth the basis for its decision; and (3) to conduct the proceedings without complying with the due process requirements of Sections 7 and 8 of the Railway Labor Act.

4. Whether the proceeding before the special board of adjustment accorded petitioner due process of law as required by the United States Constitution, apart from its noncompliance with Sections 7 and 8 of the Railway Labor Act.

STATUTES INVOLVED

The pertinent provisions of Public Law 88-108, 77 Stat. 132; 45 U.S.C. § 157 (1966 Supp.), and the Railway Labor Act, 45 U.S.C., §§ 151 ff, are set forth in Appendix D.

4

STATEMENT

Like the companion cases, Cases Nos. 499, 500, 501, and 502,[2] the instant case arises under Public Law 88-108. In Public Law 88-108, Congress required the railroads and railroad operating unions to submit their disputes over the proper manning of trains to compulsory arbitration. The manning dispute concerned "firemen on diesels" and "crew consist", i.e., the number of employees in road and yard service. It is only the crew consist issue which is involved here and not the firemen issue.

Board 282 concluded that this issue, unlike the firemen issue, could not be resolved by a nation-wide formula, but had to be resolved on a local basis. Board 282, therefore, provided for local negotiations (Award, Part III, A),[3] and, where these proved unfruitful, for the submission of disputes to special local boards of adjustment for arbitration. (Award, Part III, B).

Part III, B, established the method for calling a special board into existence, the special board's composition (a neutral referee and one representative of each party), its time limits, and the payment of expenses. As to all other procedural matters, Award 282 is completely silent.

---

[2] *Brotherhood of Railroad Trainmen v. Certain Carriers, Etc. (St. Louis Southwestern R.R.)* (No. 499); *Brotherhood of Railroad Trainmen v. Certain Carriers, Etc. (Missouri Pacific R.R.)* (No. 500); *Brotherhood of Railroad Trainmen v. Chicago, M. St. Paul & Pacific R.R.* (No. 501); *Brotherhood of Railroad Trainmen v. Certain Carriers, Etc. (Terminal Railroad Assn. of St. Louis)* (No. 502).

[3] The text of Award 282 is unofficially reported in 41 Lab. Arb. Reports 673 (1963). The relevant portion appears at J.A. 20-25.

Part III, C, sets forth the detailed and complex guidelines that the special boards were to follow in reaching their decisions. While the most important considerations in these guidelines were the "insurance of adequate safety" and the "avoidance of unreasonable [work] burdens", the guidelines also required the special boards to review each disputed job assignment in light of operating conditions, changes in operating conditions, physical characteristics of the line, the number of intersections to be protected, applicable state and municipal regulations, the presence or absence of a fireman in the engine, and the like. To apply these guidelines correctly, precise factual information was necessary; and where the facts were disputed required the special boards to sift through conflicting and partisan presentations in an effort to obtain an accurate picture of the actual conditions.

Purporting to act within this framework, Respondent, on March 30, 1964, proposed to eliminate 162 job assignments out of a total of 382 crews in 59 yards scattered through six states and to change train baggagemen assignments on 7 trains (Pltf. Ex. 2).[4]

Before Respondent sent this proposal to Petitioner on March 30, 1964, it had completed time studies on these job assignments, collected and collated data in support of its position, and had begun preparation of written submissions for presentation to the special board (R. 365).

On May 1, 1964, after four brief negotiating meetings with Petitioner, Respondent requested that a

---

[4] Petitioner below questioned whether these baggagemen assignments were covered by Award 282. This question, however, is not presented in this petition.

Special Board be convened (Pltf. Ex. 14). Although Petitioner protested that negotiations had barely begun, this request was granted on May 18 (Pltf. Ex. 17, 18).

Thus, disputes on 162 job assignments, and 7 baggagemen assignments, were submitted to the special board at a time when Respondent, but not Petitioner (which did not know in advance the job assignments that Respondent would ask the special board to eliminate), was able to present its complete position through detailed written submissions.

On May 28, 1964, Petitioner and Respondent met with the Referee to establish the hearing procedures. Despite Petitioner's protests, the Referee ordered the hearings to be held in Respondent's office and to begin on June 1, 1964. He rejected Petitioner's request that a transcript be taken, unless the Petitioner agreed to pay its full costs. As a result, no transcript of the proceeding was kept.

Starting June 1, hearings were held daily (R. 68, 164); they would begin at 9:30 a.m. and end at 4:30 p.m. There was no schedule of particular job assignments to be heard on a specific day; what cases were heard, would depend on the number already completed.

In these hearings, Petitioner had to rely on questionnaires sent to its membership (these questionnaires were intended to be a basis for the preparation of its written submissions), witnesses, and oral arguments.

The Referee denied Petitioner's repeated requests that he grant adjournments, that he view at least some of the properties,[5] and that he extend the time to file written submissions. Originally, the Referee had ruled that all written materials had to be filed with him no later than June 26, 1964. One week later, however, he ruled that all written material relating to the La-Crosse Division and Milwaukee Division had to be filed that same day; material for Milwaukee terminals had to be filed by June 17; the Twin Cities materials by June 18; and as to all other yards to be filed by June 19. June 19 was 30 days prior to the expiration of the Special Board's 60 day jurisdictional time period.

On July 10, the special board not only adopted the Respondent's position on every disputed job assignment, but copied the very language from the Company's notice including the phrase "It is proposed" (Pltf. Ex. 31, p. 18). No findings or opinion accompanied this Award.

Petitioner first challenged the Special Board's award in the United States District Court for the District of Columbia on two grounds: (1) that the Special Board procedures and the conduct of the Referee violated due process of law, and; (2) that the Award did not comply with the guidelines. This challenge was based, in part, upon undisputed conduct of the Referee and, in part, upon charges which the Referee denied. On appeal from the District Court's ruling, the Court of Appeals for the District of Columbia Circuit remanded the parties to Board 282 for that Board, in the exercise of its "primary jurisdiction", to afford Petitioner "meaningful review". *Brother-*

---

[5] Many of them were in the city where the hearings were held.

hood of Railroad Trainmen v. *Chicago, Milwaukee, St. Paul & Pac. R.R.*, 345 F. 2d 985 (D.C. Cir. 1965).

The same Court in *Brotherhood of Railroad Trainmen* v. *Certain Carriers*, 349 F. 2d 207 (D.C. Cir. 1965) remanded the question "whether or not the Special Boards of Adjustment had been required to conduct the arbitrations in compliance with Sections 7 and 8 of the Railway Labor Act."[6]

On remand, Board 282 decided that the requirements of compliance with Sections 7 and 8 "applies only to Board 282 and not to the special boards of adjustment provided for in its award." (J.A. 33). On the question of "meaningful review", it examined the record to determine whether it was sufficient to permit awards based on the guidelines and whether the BRT was afforded a full and fair hearing. On the lack of a transcript, it ruled that "a party wishing review of a decision by a special board must assume the obligation of providing a verbatim transcript . . . ." (J.A. 36)

The Court of Appeals upheld this Answer on the ground that the Court's decision which originally upheld the validity of the Award was *res judicata* on the question whether the requirements of Sections 7 and 8 of the Railway Labor Act were applicable to the Special Boards and that Petitioner was accorded a "meaningful review" by Board 282 which found no violation of due process.

---

[6] Section 4 of Public Law 88-108 provided, in pertinent part:

"To the extent not inconsistent with this joint resolution the arbitration shall be conducted pursuant to sections 7 and 8 of the Railway Labor Act, . . ."

Circuit Judge Wright dissented, as he did in *Brotherhood of Railroad Trainmen* v. *Certain Carriers, Etc. (St. Louis Southwestern R.R.) (No. 499); Brotherhood of Railroad Trainmen* v. *Certain Carriers, Etc. (Missouri Pacific R.R.) (No. 500)*, in which reviews are also being sought in this Court. In his dissent he considered that since Congress, conscious of the seriousness of its action in imposing compulsory arbitration, had provided mandatory procedural due process safeguards for the arbitration, it was inconceivable that Board 282 could delegate its arbitral authority to local boards without such safeguards being applicable to the local boards. He considered the ruling of the majority concerning *res judicata* inconsistent with the decision of the Court in *Brotherhood of Railroad Trainmen* v. *Certain Carriers, etc.*, 349 F. 2d 207 (D.C. Cir. 1965), in which case the Court, two years earlier, had, *sub silentio*, rejected the *res judicata* argument and remanded the parties to further proceedings under Public Law 88-108. He pointed out further that the Court of Appeals could not properly resolve the question of whether Petitioner was accorded due process because in violation of Section 7 of the Railway Labor Act no transcript was provided.

REASONS FOR GRANTING THE WRIT

There are three basic issues in this case, each of which calls for review by this Court. The first of these is whether Arbitration Board 282 could delegate a portion of the arbitral function conferred on it by Congress to local special boards of adjustment and relieve those local boards of the procedural requirements of Sections 7 and 8 of the Railway Labor Act which

10

requirements Congress had specified should be complied with in the arbitration proceedings. The second question calling for review by this Court is whether the unsuccessful effort by Petitioner to impeach the original award of board 282, before any of the local boards had been asked for or established and before it could be known what procedures they would believe would be applicable or what procedures they would follow, is *res judicata*, that Sections 7 and 8 were not applicable to their proceedings. The third question is whether the procedure actually followed by the special board of adjustment involved in this case denied Petitioner due process of law apart from it not complying with the procedures of Sections 7 and 8 of the Railway Labor Act.

The first two of the foregoing questions, and their importance, are the same as those questions in another petition for certiorari pending in this court filed August 16, 1967, *Brotherhood of Railroad Trainmen v. Certain Carriers, etc.,* No. 499.

The third question calling for review by this Court is almost the same as in No. 499. This is whether the procedure actually followed by the local board was a denial of constitutional due process, quite apart from its failure to comply with Sections 7 and 8 of the Railway Labor Act. In the Statement, *supra*, we have shown some respects in which due process was denied: the bias of the "neutral", the prejudicial locale of the hearings, the schedule prescribed by the "neutral" making it impossible for Petitioner to present its case, etc. As the dissenting opinion below pointed out, the violation of the requirement of Section 7 that a record be kept made it impossible to determine such issues.

The decision below is predicated primarily on the decision in *Brotherhood of Locomotive Firemen and Enginemen* v. *Chicago, B. & Q. R.R.*, 225 F. Supp. 11 (D.D.C. 1964) being *res judicata* that Sections 7 and 8 were not to govern the procedures of the local boards. In substance, this position is that at that time before there were any local boards, we should have known that the local boards would not comply with Sections 7 and 8 of the Railway Labor Act and should have known that Board 282 would later rule that such non-compliance was proper.

Nothing in Award 282 prevented the special boards from acting in conformity with the due process requirements of Sections 7 and 8[7] or prevented Board 282 from ruling that their awards were defective because they did not. At the time of the decision in *Brotherhood of Locomotive Firemen and Enginemen* v. *Chicago, B. & Q. R.R.*, *supra*, therefore, Petitioner could challenge the award only on the ground that there existed a *possibility* that the special boards would not conduct the hearings in accordance with Sections 7 and 8 of the Railway Labor Act and a *possibility* that Board 282 would interpret its Award to conflict with Public Law 88-108.

Moreover, Board 282 had explicit authority to interpret its Award. It, therefore, was in a position to interpret the Award in such a way to make it conform to the applicable statutory requirements.

If the holding below is correct, it would mean that Petitioner could have impeached Award 282 simply

---

[7] For example, Board 282 acknowledged that the special board here could have ordered a transcript (J.A. 36).

12

by showing that it was susceptible to an interpretation
which would make it unlawful, even though it was also
susceptible to interpretations that would make it lawful. A requirement that a compulsory arbitration
award can be sustained only if every possible interpretation of it would render it lawful is unnecessary
and unrealistic.

CONCLUSION

This petition for a writ of certiorari should be
granted.

Respectfully submitted,

GOLDBERG, PREVIANT & UELMEN   DAVID LEO UELMEN
211 West Wisconsin Avenue
Milwaukee, Wisconsin 53203

SCHOENE and KRAMER   MILTON KRAMER
1625 K Street, N.W.
Washington, D. C. 20006

Attorneys for Petitioner

September, 1967

APPENDIX

APPENDIX A

Opinion of the Court

The Court: This is a motion to impeach the ruling of Arbitration Board No. 282 which was in the form of answers to questions submitted to that Board in connection with the work of one of the Special Boards of Adjustment created under the basic Award.

Many of the points or objections raised are of the type that have already been discussed and disposed of by this Court in cases entitled In Re Certain Carriers etc., 231 F. Supp. 59,248 F. Supp. 1008, and Brotherhood of Railroad Trainmen v. St. Louis, Southwestern Railway Co., decided on April 21st of this year.

These objections involve such matters as whether guidelines were properly followed by the Special Board, whether it was error for the Special Board of Adjustment not to require that a transcript of the testimony be maintained unless the parties met the expense, and similar matters, and the Court without repeating the discussion refers to the discussion in the cases referred to.

There is, however, one new objection raised in this instance that was not raised in the cases already referred to, namely, that the Special Board of Adjustment did not give a fair hearing to the representatives of employees. Counsel does not point to any one circumstance which he would contend gives rise to such an inference, but he claims that an accumulation of circumstances, taken together, justify the conclusion that the hearing was not fair.

It is objected, first, that the hearing was held in premises owned by the carrier. The Court sees no basis for objection on that score.

It is further argued, and if that is sustained it would be more serious, that insufficient time was accorded for the preparation or submission of the cases. At least two months, however, expired between the service of notices under Award 282 and the hearing before the Special Board. Surely that was sufficient time for preparation. Moreover, it has been held time and time again that the question of continuance and setting dates for hearings is entirely within the discretion of the tribunal and it would be only in an extreme situation that such action would be subject to review. There is no such extreme situation here. More time was accorded for final argument than was actually used by representatives of the parties.

The Court is unable to find that there was an abuse of discretion or that the hearings were so hurried as to constitute a denial of a fair hearing.

So far as this Court is concerned, as the Court has indicated in the cases referred to, the scope of judicial review of the decision of an Arbitration Board under the Railway Labor Act is very narrow, much narrower than the scope of review of the action of an administrative agency. Considering the answers of Board 282 which are sought to be impeached in the light of the limitations contained in Section 9 of the Railway Labor Act, 45 United States Code 159, the Court concludes that the award is not vulnerable within any of the criteria set forth in the statute.

Moreover, upon reading the answers to the questions submitted to Board 282, which constitute the award involved here, it is quite evident that Board 282 examined the record and found that it was sufficient to permit awards based on the guidelines contained in Award 282, and it also reached the conclusion that the record before the Special Board was voluminous, included detailed written surveys, findings, allegations by both parties, and that there was a full and fair hearing.

This Court concludes that there is no basis for impeaching the answers made by Board 282, and, accordingly, the petition to impeach the award is dismissed.

APPENDIX B

UNITED STATES COURT OF APPEALS
FOR THE DISTRICT OF COLUMBIA CIRCUIT

No. 20,348
No. 20,349

BROTHERHOOD OF RAILROAD TRAINMEN,
APPELLANT

v.

CHICAGO, MILWAUKEE, ST. PAUL AND PACIFIC
RAILROAD COMPANY (LINES EAST), ET AL.,
APPELLEES

Appeal from the United States District Court
for the District of Columbia

Decided July 27, 1967

Mr. David Leo Uelmen, with whom *Mr. Milton Kramer* was on the brief, for appellant.

Mr. Richard T. Conway, with whom *Messers. Francis M. Shea* and *Benjamin W. Boley* were on the brief, for appellees.

Before: BASTIAN, *Senior Circuit Judge* and BURGER and WRIGHT, *Circuit Judges.*

PER CURIAM: This is another "manifestation of a litigation syndrome that seems to keep the railroads and various governmental entities in the courts on an ancient issue." *Brotherhood of Railroad Trainmen* v. *Chicago, Milwaukee, St. Paul & Pacific Railroad Co.,* — U.S. App. D.C. —, —, — F.2d —, — (Nos. 19,867, 20,003-04, decided May 19, 1967, slip op. p. 1). Issues raised in these appeals have been before this court previously in *Brotherhood of Railroad Trainmen* v. *Chicago, Milwaukee, St. Paul & Pacific Railroad Co., ibid,* and *Brotherhood of Railroad Trainmen* v. *St. Louis Southwestern Railway Co., et al.,* — U.S.

App. D.C. —, —, — F.2d — — (Nos. 20,212-13, decided May 19, 1967). Our prior opinions are controlling and dispositive of these issues and there is no need to supplement those opinions.

In addition, however, Appellant Brotherhood raises a new claim in these appeals. It now contends that the hearing before the Special Board of Adjustment did not afford it due process of law because of certain alleged procedural irregularities not heretofore considered.[1] Although these issues were exhaustively discussed and found to be without merit in Judge Robinson's original decision in the District Court, *Brotherhood of Railroad Trainmen v. Chicago, Milwaukee, St. Paul & Pacific Railroad Co.,* 237 F. Supp. 404, 418-25 (D. D.C. 1964), we remanded that case to Board 282 in order that it might pass upon these issues. *Brotherhood of Railroad Trainmen v. Chicago, Milwaukee, St. Paul & Pacific Railroad Co.,* 120 U.S. App. D.C. 295, 345 F.2d 985 (1965). The Board concluded that the alleged procedural irregularities, considered singly or together, did not deprive the B.R.T. of the minimum essentials of a full and fair hearing.

We have previously upheld the Board determination that due process was not violated by lack of a transcript; we similarily affirmed the Board decision that a "meaningful review" had been provided. Although it would appear that the specific defects raised here are subsumed within the due process concept of "meaningful review" we did not discuss them in our prior opinions. We have now fully examined the claim newly raised on this appeal, and we find it to be without merit.

Affirmed.

---

[1] Specifically the union claims that it was impossible to decide the job assignments in 60 days; that the hearing held in the company offices was inherently unfair and offered little time or space for interviews with witnesses; that there was a failure to allow a reasonable time to submit written exhibits; that the "referee" was not neutral; and that the "findings" were prepared by the company and submitted to the referee for approval.

WRIGHT, *Circuit Judge, dissenting:* Public Law 88-108[1] provides that the compulsory arbitration required in this case "shall be conducted pursuant to sections 7 and 8 of the Railway Labor Act." Pub.L. 88-108, § 4. As I have indicated in my dissents in *Brotherhood of Railroad Trainmen* v. *St. Louis Southwestern Railway Co., et al.,* Nos. 20,212-3, and *Brotherhood of Railroad Trainmen* v. *Chicago, Milwaukee, St. Paul & Pacific RR Co., et al.,* Nos. 19,867, 20,003 and 20,004, decided May 19, 1967, the Compulsory Arbitration Board convened pursuant to Public Law 88-108 cannot avoid this statutory requirement by delegating portions of its authority to local boards.

In these cases appellant makes the additional point that the local board deprived it of the minimum essentials of a full and fair hearing in that, among other things, it was denied a reasonable opportunity to prepare its case, to call witnesses, and to conduct cross-examination. The company, of course, argues that the board hearing was full and fair. Since, in violation of Section 7 of the Railway Labor Act[2] and in spite of appellant's request, no transcript of the proceedings before the local board was provided, I am unable to resolve this due process issue on this record.

I respectfully dissent.

---

[1] 77 STAT. 132 (1963), 45 U.S.C. § 157 (1964).

[2] 45 U.S.C. § 157 (1964).

6a

APPENDIX C

(Filed July 27, 1967)

Judgment

These causes came on to be heard on the record on appeal from the United States District Court for the District of Columbia, and were argued by counsel.

On Consideration Whereof, It is ordered and adjudged by this Court that the judgments of the District Court appealed from in these causes be, and they are hereby, affirmed.

Per Curiam

Separate dissenting opinion per Circuit Judge Wright.

APPENDIX D

Judicial Code

28 USC 1254 (1), 62 Stat. 928.

Cases in the courts of appeals may be reviewed by the Supreme Court by the following methods:

(1) By writ of certiorari granted upon the petition of any party to any civil or criminal case, before or after rendition of judgment or decree.

Public Law 88-108.

"Sec. 2. [Arbitration board]. There is hereby established an arbitration board to consist of seven members.

* * * * * * *

"Sec. 3. The arbitration board shall make a decision, pursuant to the procedures hereinafter set forth.

* * * * * * *

"Sec. 4. To the extent not inconsistent with this joint resolution the arbitration shall be conducted pursuant to sections 7 and 8 of the Railway Labor Act [this section and section 158 of this title], the board's award shall be made and filed as provided in said sections and shall be subject to section 9 of said Act [section 159 of this title]. The United States District Court for the District of Columbia is hereby designated as the court in which the award is to be filed, and the arbitration board shall report to the National Mediation Board in the same manner as arbitration boards functioning pursuant to the Railway Labor Act [this chapter].

* * * * * *

Railway Labor Act, Sec. 7.

Third.

* * * * * *

(b) Organization of board; procedure.

The board of arbitration shall organize and select its own chairman and make all necessary rules for conducting its hearings: *Provided, however,* That the board of arbitration shall be bound to give the parties to the controversy a full and fair hearing, which shall include an opportunity to present evidence in support of their claims, and an opportunity to present their case in person, by counsel, or by other representative as they may respectively elect.

(c) Duty to reconvene; questions considered.

Upon notice from the Mediation Board that the parties, or either party, to an arbitration desire the reconvening of the board of arbitration (or a subcommittee of such board of arbitration appointed for such purpose pursuant to the agreement to arbitrate) to pass upon any controversy over the meaning or application of their award, the board, or its subcommittee, shall at once reconvene. No question other than, or in addition to, the questions relating to the meaning or application of the award, submitted by the party or parties in writing, shall be considered by the reconvened board of arbitration or its subcommittee.

Such rulings shall be acknowledged by such board or subcommittee thereof in the same manner, and filed in the same district court clerk's office, as the original award and become a part thereof.

* * * * * * *

(e) Compensation and expenses.

Each member of any board of arbitration created under the provisions of this chapter named by either party to the arbitration shall be compensated by the party naming him. Each arbitrator selected by the arbitrators or named by the Mediation Board shall receive from the Mediation Board such compensation as the Mediation Board may fix, together with his necessary traveling expenses and expenses actually incurred for subsistence, while serving as an arbitrator.

(f) Award; disposition of original and copies.

The board of arbitration shall furnish a certified copy of its award to the respective parties to the controversy, and shall transmit the original, together with the papers and proceedings and a transcript of the evidence taken at the hearings, certified under the hands of at least a majority of the arbitrators, to the clerk of the district court of the United States for the district wherein the controversy arose or the arbitration is entered into, to be filed in said clerk's office as hereinafter provided. The said board shall also furnish a certified copy of its award, and the papers and proceedings, including testimony relating thereto, to the Mediation Board to be filed in its office; and in addition a certified copy of its award shall be filed in the office of the Interstate Commerce Commission: *Provided, however,* That such award shall not be construed to diminish or extinguish any of the powers or duties of the Interstate Commerce Commission, under the Interstate Commerce Act, as amended.

(g) Compensation of assistants to board of arbitration; expenses; quarters.

A board of arbitration may, subject to the approval of the Mediation Board, employ and fix the compensation of such assistants as it deems necessary in carrying on the arbitration proceedings. The compensation of such employees, together with their necessary traveling expenses and expenses actually incurred for subsistence, while so employed, and the necessary expenses of boards of arbitration, shall be paid by the Mediation Board.

Whenever practicable, the board shall be supplied with suitable quarters in any Federal building located at its place of meeting or at any place where the board may conduct its proceedings or deliberations.

(h) Testimony before board; oaths; attendance of witnesses; production of documents; subpoenas; compulsion of witnesses; fees.

All testimony before said board shall be given under oath or affirmation, and any member of the board shall have the power to administer oaths or affirmations. The board of arbitration, or any member thereof, shall have the power to require the attendance of witnesses and the production of such books, papers, contracts, agreements, and documents as may be deemed by the board of arbitration material to a just determination of the matters submitted to its arbitration.

* * * * * * *

Railway Labor Act, Sec. 8.

(k) Shall provide that the award of the board of arbitration and the evidence of the proceedings before the board relating thereto, when certified under the hands of at least a majority of the arbitrators, shall be filed in the clerk's office of the district court of the United States for the district wherein the controversy arose or the arbitration was entered into, which district shall be designated in the agreement; and, when so filed, such award and proceedings shall constitute the full and complete record of the arbitration;

* * * * * * *

(m) Shall provide that any difference arising as to the meaning, or the application of the provisions, of an award made by a board of arbitration shall be referred back for a ruling to the same board, or, by agreement, to a subcommittee of such board; and that such ruling, when acknowledged in the same manner, and filed in the same district court clerk's office, as the original award, shall be a part of and shall have the same force and effect as such original award; and

* * * * * * *

IN THE
SUPREME COURT OF THE UNITED STATES
OCTOBER TERM, 1967

No. 620

BROTHERHOOD OF RAILROAD TRAINMEN,
Petitioner,

v.

CHICAGO, MILWAUKEE, ST. PAUL & PACIFIC RAILROAD COMPANY, ET AL., *Respondents.*

ON PETITION FOR A WRIT OF CERTIORARI TO THE UNITED STATES
COURT OF APPEALS FOR THE DISTRICT OF COLUMBIA CIRCUIT

BRIEF FOR RESPONDENT CHICAGO, MILWAUKEE, ST. PAUL & PACIFIC RAILROAD COMPANY IN OPPOSITION.

JAMES P. REEDY
  Union Station Building
  Chicago, Illinois 60606

SHEA & GARDNER
  734 Fifteenth St., N.W.
  Washington, D.C.

Of Counsel

FRANCIS M. SHEA
RICHARD T. CONWAY
BENJAMIN W. BOLEY
  734 Fifteenth St., N.W.
  Washington, D.C. 20005

JAMES R. WOLFE
CHARLES I. HOPKINS, JR.
  Union Station Building
  Chicago, Illinois 60606
*Attorneys for Respondent
Chicago, Milwaukee, St. Paul &
Pacific Railroad Company*

INDEX

TABLE OF CONTENTS

TABLE OF CITATIONS

Cases:

No. 620

BROTHERHOOD OF RAILROAD TRAINMEN,
Petitioner,

v.

CHICAGO, MILWAUKEE, ST. PAUL & PACIFIC
RAILROAD COMPANY, ET AL., *Respondents.*

ON PETITION FOR A WRIT OF CERTIORARI TO THE UNITED STATES
COURT OF APPEALS FOR THE DISTRICT OF COLUMBIA CIRCUIT

BRIEF FOR RESPONDENT CHICAGO, MILWAUKEE, ST. PAUL & PACIFIC RAILROAD COMPANY IN OPPOSITION.

Opinions Below

The opinion of the Court of Appeals (App. B of Petition), not yet officially reported, is unofficially reported at 56 CCH Labor Cases ¶12,090. The opinion of the District Court (App. A of Petition) has not been reported.

Jurisdiction

The jurisdictional requisites are adequately set forth in the petition.

Question Presented

Whether the answer by Arbitration Board No. 282 to BRT Questions No. 32(a) and (b), that a special board of adjust-

(1)

ment established under Arbitration Award No. 282 did not deprive petitioner of the minimum essentials of a full and fair hearing, may be impeached under Section 9 of the Railway Labor Act as incorporated into Public Law 88-108 on the ground that the special board of adjustment was required by statute or by the due process clause of the Fifth Amendment to the Constitution to provide petitioner with a free transcript of its proceedings?

Statement of the Case

In November of 1959, most of the nation's Class I railroads served five unions (including petitioner) with notices under Section 6 of the Railway Labor Act (45 U.S.C. §156) of proposed changes in a number of obsolete rules which were causing serious overmanning of trains. One of the proposals thus made was to abolish all rules requiring the use of trainmen (such as brakemen and helpers) in road and yard service, and to permit management in its discretion to determine the number of such trainmen to be used. In September of 1960, the unions served the railroads (including this respondent) with Section 6 notices of various counterproposals, including a proposal by petitioner to establish a rule requiring the use of at least two trainmen on all crews in road and yard service. The parties exhausted the "major" dispute procedures of the Railway Labor Act (45 U.S.C. §§151-160) without settling this dispute, and thus were in a position to resort to self help including strikes by the unions. See *Locomotive Engineers v. B. & O. R. Co.*, 372 U.S. 284 (1963).

To prevent such a disaster, Congress enacted P.L. 88-108 (77 Stat. 132). That statute committed the crew-consist issue raised by those aspects of the Section 6 notices referred to above and another issue involving the use of locomotive firemen to final and binding arbitration by an arbitration board commonly known at Arbitration Board No. 282.

Section III of the Award (JA 20-25) by Arbitration Board No. 282 related to the crew-consist issue. It provided, among other things, that no change could be made in existing rules requiring a stipulated number of trainmen to be used on crews in road and yard service except by agreement or pursuant to the procedures established by the Award. In general, those procedures permitted either a carrier or a union to serve the other with written notice of proposed changes in rules requiring a stipulated number of trainmen, provided that they should confer and attempt to reach agreement upon such proposals in the light of "guidelines" or standards specified in the Award, and provided that, if no agreement was reached, the dispute could be submitted by either party to a special board of adjustment (composed of one representative of the carrier, one representative of the union and a neutral member) for final decision, pursuant to those guidelines.

Petitioner and three other unions filed petitions to impeach the Award, pursuant to Section 9 of the Railway Labor Act (45 U.S.C. §159) as incorporated by Section 4 of P.L. 88-108, contending that the Award did not comply with P.L. 88-108, was unconstitutional and was otherwise invalid. The validity of the Award was upheld, however, in a decision that has become final. *Brotherhood of Loc. Fire. & Eng.* v. *Chicago, B. & Q. R. Co.*, 225 F. Supp. 11 (D. D.C., 1964), aff'd *per curiam*, 331 F.2d 1020 (D.C. Cir., 1964), cert. den., 377 U.S. 918 (1964).

The crew-consist provisions of the Award became effective on January 25, 1964. On March 10, 1964, this respondent served petitioner with two written notices under Article III of the Award proposing to change from two to one the stipulated number of helpers on 162 yard assignments and to eliminate the baggageman on seven passenger trains. After negotiations between the parties failed to bring about an agreement, respondent requested the establishment of a special board of adjustment with respect to the baggagemen notice on April 21, 1964 and with respect to the yard-crew notice on May 1, 1964. A special board of adjustment was established to hear the dispute, on May 18, 1964, when the neutral member was appointed by the National Mediation Board. Section III-B(3) of the Award provides (JA 22) that: "Decisions of the special board of adjustment shall be rendered within 60 days after the appointment of the neutral member."

The special board of adjustment held an organizational meeting on May 28, 1964, and commenced its hearings on June 1, 1964. During the meeting on May 28, petitioner asked whether a transcript of the proceedings would be made, and was informed that it could have one made at its own expense, if it wished. Neither party arranged for a transcript to be made. The hearings continued on every week day until June 29, 1964, except for June 3 and 4 and part of June 17. Shortly after receiving respondent's notices of March 10, 1964, petitioner distributed questionnaires to its members who worked on the crews involved concerning the operation of those crews. No further effort was made by petitioner to prepare for the hearings until the initial meeting of the special board on May 28, 1964. Nevertheless, petitioner submitted more than 400 completed questionnaires and presented testimony by live witnesses relating to practically every assignment at issue. Extensive written and oral evidence also was submitted by this respondent. The special board allowed four days, between June 29 and July 2, 1964, for oral argument, but such argument was waived by the parties.

The special board of adjustment issued its awards on July 10, 1964. Thereupon, petitioner filed an action in the United States District Court for the District of Columbia to enjoin this respondent from putting the awards into effect. Numerous issues were raised, most of which concerned the fairness of the hearing before the special board, including a contention that petitioner was deprived of due process of law because the special board did not have its proceedings transcribed and make a transcript available without cost to petitioner. After an extensive trial before the Honorable Spottswood W. Robinson, III, the complaint was dismissed on the merits in accordance with findings and conclusions reported in *Brotherhood of Railroad Train.* v. *Chicago, M., St. P. & P. R. Co.*, 237 F. Supp. 404 (D. D.C., 1964).[1] Upon appeal by petitioner, the judgment in that case was vacated and the case was remanded "with instructions to dismiss the complaint without prejudice to such further application to Board 282 as any party may choose to make." *Brotherhood of Railroad Train.* v. *Chicago, M., St. P. & P. R. Co.*, 345 F.2d 985, 988 (D.C. Cir., 1965). In essence, the Court of Appeals held that the complaint raised issues which were within the jurisdiction of Arbitration Board No. 282 to decide, pursuant to Section 8(m) of the Railway Labor Act (45 U.S.C. §158(m)) as incorporated by Section 4 of P.L. 88-108.

Following the remand, petitioner submitted several questions to Board 282, including those denominated as BRT Questions No. 32(a) and (b), which read as follows (JA 36-37):

"(a) Whether the Awards issued by Referee K. P. O'Gallagher, which permitted the Chicago, Milwaukee, St. Paul & Pacific Railroad Company to reduce the crews on 162 out of 312 job assignments plus eliminate

---

[1] The record compiled before Judge Robinson was made available, by stipulation of the parties, to Board 282 in connection with its consideration of BRT Questions No. 32 (a) and (b), and to the lower courts in connection with their consideration of the petition to impeach those answers. The factual statements made in the foregoing paragraphs of this Statement of the Case are based upon that record, unless otherwise indicated.

seven baggagemen assignments, followed the guidelines established by Board 282.

"(b) Whether the hearing conducted before the Special Board of Adjustment appointed by the National Mediation Board pursuant to Public Law 88-108, Referee K. P. O'Gallagher presiding, was held under circumstances that deprived the BRT of procedural due process of law, thus nullifying the awards."

On December 12, 1965, Board 282 answered those questions together, as follows (JA 37):

"To answer these questions and to provide 'meaningful review' as we have defined that term in our Preliminary Statement in respect to B.R.T. Questions 32, 33, and 36, we have examined the entire record made before Judge Robinson. This record consists of all of the exhibits submitted to the Special Board of Adjustment and the referee's notes, plus oral arguments made by counsel to Judge Robinson. In addition, we have had the benefit of oral and written arguments made by counsel to Arbitration Board 282. As explained in our Preliminary Statement, we think it outside the boundaries of 'meaningful review' to pass judgment on the merits of these awards. Rather, we have examined the record to determine whether it was sufficient to permit awards based on the guidelines and whether the B.R.T. was afforded a full and fair hearing. The record is voluminous; it includes detailed written surveys, findings, and allegations by both parties in respect to all the jobs covered by the carrier's notice. The referee asserted that the awards were based on the guidelines, and he so testified before Judge Robinson. We can find nothing in the record which would justify a conclusion that the awards were governed by any other considerations.

"On the question whether the B.R.T. was denied a

full and fair hearing, we conclude from our study of the record that the alleged procedural irregularities, considered singly or together, did not deprive the B.R.T. of the minimum essentials of a full and fair hearing.''

In the Preliminary Statement in respect to BRT Questions No. 32, 33 and 36, issued on October 10, 1965 and referred to in the above quoted answer to BRT Questions No. 32(a) and (b), Board 282 stated, among other things, that (JA 34-36):

"At the outset, we wish to emphasize that, in our judgment, a 'meaningful review' in the context of Award 282 is not a trial de novo. As we have repeatedly stated, our purpose in providing for special boards of adjustment was to bring about prompt and final settlement of disputes over crew consists. We recognized that these disputes were complex and varied, and that they could be equitably resolved only after a careful and detailed examination of local conditions and the application of the guidelines laid down in the Award. A trial de novo, following an appeal to Board 282 from the decision of a special board, would thus defeat the entire purpose of our decision.

* * * * * * *

"In our judgment the applicable standards in this case are those specified in Award 282, and 'meaningful review' involves neither more nor less than a determination whether a challenged decision by a special board has followed the procedures and applied the guidelines set forth in Section III, Parts A, B, and C, of that Award.

* * * * * * *

"... Moreover, we deem it incumbent upon any party

seeking a meaningful review of the decision of a special board to make such review possible ... by providing us with an adequate record .... By the same token, a party wishing review of a decision by a special board must assume the obligation of providing a verbatim transcript or other satisfactory evidence of the proceedings before that board. If the opposing party refuses to share the cost of a transcript, and the neutral arbitrator determines, in the exercise of his discretion, that a transcript is unnecessary, the party desiring one is nevertheless entitled to have it; but with that right comes the obligation to pay the cost.''

A petition to impeach the answers to BRT Questions No. 32(a) and (b) was filed by petitioner, pursuant to Section 9 of the Railway Labor Act as incorporated by Section 4 of P.L. 88-108, in the United States District Court for the District of Columbia (JA 3-13). In an order entered on July 11, 1966, that petition was dismissed by the Honorable Alexander Holtzoff (JA 40), pursuant to an opinion (JA 38-39) in which he concluded, among other things, that the ''Court is unable to find that there was an abuse of discretion or that the hearings were so hurried as to constitute a denial of a fair hearing.''

The United States Court of Appeals for the District of Columbia Circuit affirmed, in an opinion issued on July 27, 1967. After noting that petitioner's contentions based upon the failure of the special board of adjustment to provide it with a free transcript of the proceedings before the special board had been disposed of adversely to petitioner in earlier decisions ''which are controlling and dispositive of these issues'' (Pet., App. B, at 4a), the Court held petitioner's contention that it had been deprived of a fair hearing before the special board ''to be without merit'' (Pet., App. B, at 4a).

The prior decisions thus referred to by the Court of Appeals are its decisions in *Brotherhood of Railroad Trainmen* v. *Chicago, Milwaukee, St. Paul & Pacific Railroad Co.*, — F.2d —, 55 CCH Labor Cases ¶11,931 (May 19, 1967), petition for writ of certiorari pending, No. 500 (O. T. 1967), and in *Brotherhood of Railroad Trainmen* v. *St. Louis Southwestern Railway Co.*, — F.2d —, 55 CCH Labor Cases ¶11,928 (May 19, 1967), petition for writ of certiorari pending, No. 499 (O.T. 1967). In those cases, the Court of Appeals affirmed the denial of petitions by the Brotherhood of Railroad Trainmen to impeach the answers to BRT Questions No. 32(c) and (d), 33, 36 and 47.[2] Board 282 ruled, in answer to BRT Questions No. 36 and 47, that its Award did not require the special boards of adjustment to make transcripts of their proceedings or otherwise to follow the procedures specified in Sections 7 and 8 of the Railway Labor Act (45 U.S.C. §§ 157, 158), although a party to a special board proceeding was entitled to have a transcript made at its own expense if it so desired. The Brotherhood of Railroad Trainmen contended that Award 282 as so interpreted is invalid because it did not comply with the provision in Section 4 of P.L. 88-108 requiring Board 282 to follow the procedures specified in Sections 7 and 8 of the Railway Labor Act and also because the special boards had to make a transcript of their proceedings in order to comply with the due process clause of the Fifth Amendment

---

[2] The decision with respect to the answer to BRT Question No. 36 is before this Court on petition for writ of certiorari in No. 500, and the decision with respect to the answer to BRT Question No. 47 is before this Court on petition for writ of certiorari in No. 499. Neither the answers to those questions nor the petitions in Nos. 499 and 500 involve this respondent. The decision with respect to the answer to BRT Question No. 33 is before this Court on petition for writ of certiorari in No. 501. While that answer and petition does involve this respondent, the issues are not related to the issues in this case. This Court has not been requested to review the decision with respect to the answers to BRT Questions No. 32(c) and (d), which answers also involved this respondent.

to the Constitution.[3] The Court of Appeals held that those contentions were foreclosed by the doctrine of *res judicata* since they could have been raised in the proceeding to impeach the validity of Award 282 which was decided adversely to the Brotherhood in a decision which became final in 1964 (see p. 3, *supra*).

Argument

All of petitioner's arguments basically are grounded upon a contention that the Award by Arbitration Board No. 282 is invalid because it has been interpreted by the Board as not requiring the special boards of adjustment to make a transcript of their proceedings or otherwise to comply with the procedural requirements of Sections 7 and 8 (45 U.S.C. §§ 157 and 158) of the Railway Labor Act. However, BRT Questions No. 32(a) and (b)—the only questions here involved—did *not* raise that issue and the Award was *not* so interpreted by Board 282 in answer to them. See pp. 5-7, *supra*. That issue *was* raised and the Award *was* so interpreted in BRT Questions No. 36 and 47. Judgments affirming the dismissal of petitions to impeach the answers to those questions are now pending in this Court as Nos. 499 and 500 (see p. 9, *supra*). But whatever may be the outcome of those cases, the answers to BRT Questions No. 32(a) and (b) plainly cannot be impeached upon a ground which is not raised by those answers.

Petitioner did inquire, in BRT Question No. 32(b), as to whether the hearings before the special board of adjustment were "held under circumstances that deprived the

---

[3] While the Court of Appeals did not deem a discussion of the due process issue to be necessary in its prior decisions and that issue is not raised by the petitions in Nos. 499 and 500, that issue was raised before the Court of Appeals in those cases and necessarily was disposed of by the Court's decisions. Thus, in its opinion in this case, the Court of Appeals noted that it had "previously upheld the Board determination that due process was not violated by lack of a transcript . . . ." Pet., App. B, at 4a.

BRT of procedural due process of law," to which Board
282 responded that: "On the question whether the B.R.T.
was denied a full and fair hearing, we conclude from our
study of the record that the alleged procedural irregularities, considered singly or together, did not deprive the
B.R.T. of the minimum essentials of a full and fair hearing." [4] See pp. 5-7, *supra*. One of the alleged "procedural
irregularities" which petitioner contended deprived it of
"procedural due process of law" was the failure of the
special board to have its proceedings transcribed and to
make the transcript available without cost to petitioner.
To the extent that petitioner is contending that a free transcript is essential to "a full and fair hearing" so as to
accord it procedural due process of law as commanded by
the Fifth Amendment to the Constitution, an issue which
is involved in this case is presented.

This issue, however, is completely lacking in substance.
Petitioner was informed by the special board that it could
have the proceedings of the special board transcribed at
petitioner's own expense, if it chose to do so. Petitioner
elected not to exercise that right. Thus, petitioner's contention necessarily comes down to the proposition that it has
a constitutional due process right to a *free* transcript of
the special board proceedings. This Court has held, of
course, that a pauper has a constitutional right to a free
transcript in some circumstances. *E.g., Griffin* v. *Illinois*,
351 U.S. 12 (1956). But petitioner does not claim to be a
pauper, and neither this Court nor any other court of which
we are aware has held that a non-pauper has a constitu-

---

[4] In its Preliminary Statement of October 10, 1965, Board 282 noted
(JA 35) that whether or not "a party has been deprived of due process
in the constitutional sense is, of course, a question for the courts," but its
review jurisdiction over the awards of special boards of adjustment included jurisdiction to determine "whether either party to a proceeding before
a special board was deprived of a full and fair hearing, as that concept is
normally understood and applied to ad hoc arbitration proceedings."

tional right to a free transcript. Indeed, it is recognized that a party to an arbitration proceeding ordinarily has no right of any kind to a transcript of the proceedings, absent a statutory requirement or agreement to the contrary. *Bernhardt* v. *Polygraphic Co.*, 350 U.S. 198, 203-204, fn. 4 (1956); *Petition of Brink*, 98 F. Supp. 135, 137-138 (E.D. N.Y., 1951), aff'd, 193 F.2d 1009 (2d Cir., 1952); *Commercial Solvents Corp.* v. *Louisiana Liquid F. Co.*, 20 F.R.D. 359, 362 (S.D. N.Y., 1957). In the federal district courts, a party is entitled to a transcript of a proceeding only when he has "request[ed]" one to be made by the court reporter and "has agreed to pay the fee therefor . . .," 28 U.S.C. § 753(b), unless he is a pauper or a transcript has been ordered by the court.[5]

In any event, the court below held that petitioner is foreclosed by the doctrine of *res judicata* from raising the contention that the Award is invalid, either by reason of Sections 7 and 8 of the Railway Labor Act or by reason of the due process clause, because it does not require the special boards of adjustment to transcribe their proceedings and make the transcript available to petitioner without cost. As we have noted (pp. 8-10, *supra*), the court relied upon two of its prior decisions for that holding, which decisions are now before this Court on petitions for writ of certiorari in Nos. 499 and 500.

In the instant petition, petitioner does not assert any reason as to why this Court should review that holding, other than to state that the questions relating thereto (and to the issue on the merits as to whether Sections 7 and 8 are applicable to the proceedings of the special boards), "and their importance, are the same as those questions in another

---

[5] Court reporters are now provided pursuant to 28 U.S.C. §753. Prior to the enactment of that statute, however, a party who desired a transcript had to see that a stenographer was present as well as pay for the transcript. *Coulston* v. *United States*, 51 F.2d 178, 180 (10th Cir., 1931).

petition for writ of certiorari pending in this court filed August 16, 1967, *Brotherhood of Railroad Trainmen* v. *Certain Carriers, etc.*, No 499'' (Pet., at 10). We think it sufficient, therefore, merely to adopt and incorporate by reference the briefs of the respondent carriers in opposition to the petitions in Nos. 499 and 500, insofar as those briefs relate to the *res judicata* issue, including the demonstration therein that neither P.L. 88-108 nor the Award required the special boards of adjustment to comply with the procedural requirements of Sections 7 and 8 of the Railway Labor Act.[6]

Petitioner also requests this Court to determine ''whether the procedure actually followed by the local board was a denial of constitutional due process,'' because of alleged bias of the neutral member, the locale of the hearings and the time schedule for the hearings, but inconsistently asserts that the absence of a transcript of the special board's proceedings makes ''it impossible to determine such issues'' (Pet., at 10).

As pointed out above, petitioner could have had a transcript of the special board's proceedings if it had been willing to pay for one. To the extent that the absence of a transcript prevents review of those proceedings, therefore, that is a chance which petitioner took when it elected not

---

[6] Brief in Opposition for Respondents Missouri Pacific Railroad Company, Natchez & Southern Railway Company and The Texas & Pacific Railway Company (No. 500), and Brief in Opposition for Respondent St. Louis Southwestern Railway Company (No. 499), the latter of which adopts and incorporates by reference the arguments in the former brief. The petitions in those cases did not raise the due process issue (although it was raised in those cases below), see fn. 3, at p. 10, *supra*, so the briefs in opposition do not discuss the application of the *res judicata* doctrine to that issue. It is well established, however, that that doctrine applies to constitutional issues as well as to other issues, including the rule that a party is precluded from raising in a second suit an issue which was not raised in an earlier suit asserting the same cause of action. *Chicot County Dist.* v. *Bank.* 308 U.S. 371 (1940).

to exercise its right to arrange for a transcript. Insofar as we are aware, the view expressed by Board 282 that a party who desires review of the decision of a special board has an obligation to "make such review possible . . . by providing us with an adequate record" (see p. 8, *supra*) accords with the universal practice of appellate courts. This Court, for example, requires a petitioner for a writ of certiorari to file "a transcript of the record in the case . . ." (Rule 21(1) of the Supreme Court).

Secondly, a record for purposes of review can be prepared by means other than a stenographic transcript. See, *e.g.*, *Herring* v. *Kennedy-Herring Hardware Company*, 261 F.2d 202, 203 (6th Cir., 1958); *Cadby* v. *Savoretti*, 242 F.2d 751 (5th Cir., 1957). Rule 75(c) F.R.Civ.P., for example, provides a means for preparing a record on appeal when "no report of the evidence or proceedings at a hearing or trial was made, or if a transcript is unavailable. . . ." In the past, it was common for review to be had on a bill of exceptions which did "not embody a verbatim transcript of the evidence but, on the contrary, a statement with respect to the evidence adequate to present the contentions made in the appellate court." *Miller* v. *United States*, 317 U.S. 192, 198 (1942).

Thirdly, an extensive record of the occurrences during the special board's proceedings and of related matters was compiled in the trial before Judge Robinson in the District Court. See p. 5, *supra*. Upon the basis of that record, Judge Robinson was able to make comprehensive findings of fact and to conclude that petitioner's various allegations are groundless both in fact and in law, including its allegations that the neutral member was biased (237 F. Supp., at 424), that the locale of the hearings was prejudicial (237 F. Supp., at 422-423), and that the time schedule for the hearings allowed petitioner inadequate time to prepare (237 F. Supp., at 419-422). By stipulation of the parties, the record thus compiled before Judge Robinson was made available to Board 282 for use in its consideration of BRT Questions No. 32(a) and (b), and to the courts below for use in their consideration of the petition to impeach the Board's answer to those questions, and all of those tribunals concluded that petitioner had received a fair hearing. See pp. 5-10, *supra*.

Finally, no attempt has been made in the petition to show that the judgment of the court below is erroneous insofar as it relates to this aspect of the case, or that there is a conflict with a decision of this Court or of some other court of appeals. It is plain, moreover, that at most no more is involved than a determination of the facts in a particular case and the application of settled concepts of law to those particular facts. We submit, therefore, that the issue on the merits of petitioner's due process contentions does not call for an exercise of this Court's discretionary certiorari jurisdiction, particularly in view of the fact that all of the tribunals below which considered the issue, including Board 282, concluded that petitioner received a fair hearing before the special board of adjustment.

Conclusion

For the reasons stated above, the petition for writ of certiorari should be denied.

Respectfully submitted,

JAMES P. REEDY
  Union Station Building
  Chicago, Illinois 60606

SHEA & GARDNER
  734 Fifteenth St., N.W.
  Washington, D.C.

Of Counsel

FRANCIS M. SHEA
RICHARD T. CONWAY
BENJAMIN W. BOLEY
  734 Fifteenth St., N.W.
  Washington, D.C. 20005

JAMES R. WOLFE
CHARLES I. HOPKINS, JR.
  Union Station Building
  Chicago, Illinois 60606

*Attorneys for Respondent
Chicago, Milwaukee, St. Paul &
Pacific Railroad Company*

(2677-3)

No. 620

In the Supreme Court of the United States

OCTOBER TERM, 1967

BROTHERHOOD OF RAILROAD TRAINMEN, PETITIONER

v.

CHICAGO, MILWAUKEE, ST. PAUL, AND PACIFIC
RAILROAD COMPANY, ET AL.

ON PETITION FOR A WRIT OF CERTIORARI TO THE UNITED
STATES COURT OF APPEALS FOR THE DISTRICT OF COLUMBIA
CIRCUIT

MEMORANDUM FOR RALPH T. SEWARD IN OPPOSITION

RALPH S. SPRITZER,
Acting Solicitor General,
Department of Justice,
Washington, D.C. 20530.

In the Supreme Court of the United States

OCTOBER TERM, 1967

No. 620

BROTHERHOOD OF RAILROAD TRAINMEN, PETITIONER

v.

CHICAGO, MILWAUKEE, ST. PAUL, AND PACIFIC
RAILROAD COMPANY, ET AL.

*ON PETITION FOR A WRIT OF CERTIORARI TO THE UNITED
STATES COURT OF APPEALS FOR THE DISTRICT OF COLUMBIA
CIRCUIT*

MEMORANDUM FOR RALPH T. SEWARD IN OPPOSITION

Petitioner here presents the same questions, arising in the same context, as those it presented in *Brotherhood of Railroad Trainmen* v. *Certain Carriers*, Nos. 499 and 500, this Term. For the reasons set forth in our brief in opposition in Nos. 499 and 500, we believe that the petition for a writ of certiorari should be denied.

Respectfully submitted.

RALPH S. SPRITZER,
Acting Solicitor General.

OCTOBER 1967.

(1)

U.S. GOVERNMENT PRINTING OFFICE: 1967